Nimble Books LLC

# Bestiary of Intelligence Writing

## Enhanced with Text Analytics by PageKicker Robot Phil_73

Also by PageKicker Robot Phil_73

A Christmas Carol: Enhanced with Text Analytics and Content by PageKicker Robot Phil_73
*Bitcoin test book*
Complementary Info to CBInsight's 2015 Tech IPO Pipeline Report
OWASP Top 10: The Top 10 Most Critical Web Application Security Threats: Enhanced with Text Analytics and Content by PageKicker Robot Phil_73

## Publishing Information

Nimble Books LLC
wfz@nimblebooks.com
1521 Martha Avenue, Ann Arbor, Michigan, USA 48103

## About the Robot Author

## Phil_73

This book was assembled with pride by PageKicker robot **Phil 73**. Phil was born in the year 3019 of the Third Age and lives in Hobbiton, the Shire. His hobbies include rock climbing, listening to jazz, and tagging crowd-sourced images.

# Acknowledgements

I'd like to thank the enabling technologies that make me possible, including Bitnami, calibre, fbcmd, Magento, mySQL, nltk, pandoc, poppler, spyder, ttytter, and Ubuntu.
I'd also like to thank the people at PageKicker including Ken Leith, Brian Smiga, and Fred Zimmerman.

# Programmatically Generated Summary

Approved for Release: 2014/07/29 C00619161 ....

63 Approved for Release: 2014/07/29 C00619161 Approved for Release: 2014/07/29 C00619161 Bestiary Heightened tensions are easily recognized by their elongated shapeconventional tensions teetering about on stilts.

70 Approved for Release: 2014/07/29 C00619161 Approved for Release: 2014/07/29 C00619161 Bestiary ,

# Readability Report

Flesh-Kincaid Grade Level: 13.34
Flesh Reading Ease Score: 33.58
Sentences: 155
Words: 2,971
Average Syllables per Word: 1.82
Average Words per Sentence: 19.17

## *Explanation*

The Flesch/Flesch–Kincaid readability tests are designed to indicate comprehension difficulty when reading a passage of contemporary academic English. There are two tests: the Flesch Reading Ease and the Flesch–Kincaid Grade Level. Although they use the same core measures (word length and sentence length), they have different weighting factors. The results of the two tests correlate approximately inversely: a text with a comparatively high score on the Reading Ease test should have a lower score on the Grade Level test. Rudolf Flesch devised both systems while J. Peter Kincaid developed the latter for the United States Navy.

The Flesch-Kincaid grade level corresponds to a US education grade level, where higher grades are expected to understand more challenging material.

In the Flesch Reading Ease test, higher scores indicate material that is easier to read. Typical scores: Reader's Digest 65, Time Magazine 52, Harvard Law Review 30.

There is a good discussion at
http://en.wikipedia.org/wiki/Flesch%E2%80%93Kincaid_readability_test.
\newpage

# Unique Proper Nouns and Key Terms

analyst
CIA
Dr. Rube Goldberg
ernments
Eugene McCarthy
Europe
forecaster
Gregor Mendel
Headquarters Building
Hegel
Intelligence Agency
Intelligence Writing
James
Jeff
Kilpatrick
Marx
McNamara
mortality rate
North America
official
Pentagon
political analyst
principal
school of psychoanalysis
Secretary
straints
strait.
supervisor
two decades
US
US Government
WorldWar II

TITLE:   Bestiary of Intelligence Writing

AUTHOR:   (b)(3)(c)

Drawings by   (b)(3)(c)

VOLUME:   26   ISSUE:   Fall   YEAR:   1982

# STUDIES IN INTELLIGENCE

A collection of articles on the historical, operational, doctrinal, and theoretical aspects of intelligence.

All statements of fact, opinion or analysis expressed in Studies in Intelligence are those of the authors. They do not necessarily reflect official positions or views of the Central Intelligence Agency or any other US Government entity, past or present. Nothing in the contents should be construed as asserting or implying US Government endorsement of an article's factual statements and interpretations.

*Confusion is probably
almost inevitable*

# BESTIARY OF INTELLIGENCE WRITING *

(b)(3)(c)

Drawings by        (b)(3)(c)

Older employees may recall that when the Headquarters Building was being constructed, guard dogs stalked the corridors by night to sniff out trespassers. Practically no one is aware, however, of the collection of strange fauna in a corner of a sub-basement, the location of which must remain secret. This collection, known as the Bestiary of Intelligence Writing, consists of specimen samples of cliches and misused or overused word combinations that CIA editors have encountered frequently over the years.

Now, for the first time, the Curator of the Collection has received permission to reveal the existence of the Bestiary and identify some of its principal specimens for the enlightenment, education, and general edification of CIA writers. It is hoped that with their new awareness of the Bestiary, analysts and other authors will keep their eyes peeled, noses to the grindstone, and ears to the ground, to call the attention of editors to other candidates for possible inclusion in the collection.

### The Collection

1. Multidisciplinary analysis
2. Viable alternatives
3. Mounting crises
4. Parameters
5. Heightened tensions
6. Dire straits
7. Far-reaching implication
8. Available evidence
9. Foreseeable future
10. Almost inevitable
11. Nonstarter
12. Economic constraints
13. Broad outlines
14. Net effect
15. Overwhelming majority

* Apologies to *A Political Bestiary*, by Eugene McCarthy, James J. Kilpatrick, and Jeff MacNelly.

59

Multidisciplinary analysis, once a euphemism for the school of psycho-analysis whose treatment utilizes certain perversions, has gained new respectability since being applied to intelligence zoology. In this animal world, the multidisciplinary analysis has been around for years but has only recently been "discovered" as a species separate from other kinds of analysis.[*] A multidisciplinary analysis looks like two or more conventional one-dimensional analyses welded together. It appears rather unkempt, with lots of loose ends hanging here and there, and its surfaces have a sticky substance that allows extraneous materials to adhere. Because of its variegated aspect, it appears to have more depth than its one-dimensional cousins.

Multidisciplinary analysis has begun to flourish to an unprecedented degree in recent months and has largely swept its conventional cousins into the trash bin of history. Some who prefer the clean lines of conventional analysis are not certain this trend is a good thing. Multidisciplinary analysis heretofore was a hybrid, the fruit of the casual mating of standard forms of analysis; some scientists doubt the survivability of a multidisciplinary analysis arrived at through forced breeding. Others argue that multidisciplinary analysis is the wave of the future ("Ordnung und Multidiziplin muessen sein!") and proclaim that it is really something more (Ueberanalyse) than the sum of its parts.

---

[*] Zoological historians disagree over where multidisciplinary analysis first appeared, but most believe it evolved in North America in the second half of the twentieth century. Some believe that Dr. Rube Goldberg was its Gregor Mendel.

60

*Bestiary*

Viable alternatives, nature's born troubleshooters, are moody and shy. They wander off when times are good because governments and officials tend to ignore them; when times are bad, officials are dismayed to discover that they don't have any. Analysts sometimes confuse viable alternatives with their

more common cousins, plain alternatives, which often tempt troubled officials with false solutions. Unlike viable alternatives, regular alternatives are less shy and never go away, even when officials continually reject them. Officials as well as analysts often cannot differentiate between the two sub-species until their advice has been tried and judged.

No one has discovered the origin of viable alternatives. Some scientists believe their propagation is by parthenogenesis because viable alternatives tend to be mutually exclusive and have never been known to mate. Others suspect that viable alternatives may be related to problems because problems occasionally suggest viable alternatives.

There is even learned disagreement over the origin of the word "viable." Novice analysts often believe the word derives from and combines with the Latin *via*, meaning *by way of*, and *bull*. Others see the Latin root as modifying the noun in the sense of, in this case, an alternative that succeeds. But this imparts a whiff of ex-post-factoism unworthy of the true analyst. Experienced analysts avoid the issue.

61

*Bestiary*

Mounting crises are frequently detected by intelligence analysts, but genuine crises are rare, and most sightings probably are of the larval form, known as problems and difficulties.[*] Most crises are of the political or economic gender, but occasionally the sighting of a military (or of an even rarer, social) crisis is claimed. Crises tend to shun each other's company, although political and economic crises sometimes go hand in hand. Because they are almost impossible to identify when young (chicken sexers have the best record) and grow slowly, crises are almost always seen as mounting. They are never observed dismounting, and their decease remains an enigma to analysts. There is considerable non-scientific thinking about how they end their days: some believe that crises disappear, dissolve, evaporate, or "are resolved."

---

[*] Learned literature is not wholly agreed that problems and difficulties are a larval form of crises. There appears to be an ample body of evidence that problems and difficulties can develop into crises, but it is equally obvious that not all do so. Some observers argue, in fact, that crises must be a separate species because while governments never want to have crises around, they appear, for some reason, to tolerate problems and difficulties, perhaps to create an image of activity and a raison d'etre.

62

*Bestiary*

Parameters, beloved of defense specialists and bureaucrats in general, are the watchdogs of analysts who like to think "big thoughts." Legless creatures, parameters must be "established" by the analyst, who typically places them at the fringes of activity, more to keep the activity from straying than to prevent infiltration from the outside.

Parameters are the next evolutionary development of limits, which have existed for centuries but which tend to be common, colorless, and susceptible to over-extension. Some of the supposed greater deterrent effect of parameters stems from the awe they inspire in the analyst and, he hopes, in the reader. Because no one—until this writing—was sure what parameters were, people have been content to observe them, once in place, rather than to challenge them.

As their name suggests, parameters invariably exist as pairs; a solitary unimeter does not exist in nature. Their method of reproduction is somewhat obscure; they are probably androgynous but are never heard of until somebody "sets" them. Nor is their decease well understood: once they are "set," they are never unset, and they apparently are left in place to be forgotten.

63

*Bestiary*

Heightened tensions are easily recognized by their elongated shape—conventional tensions teetering about on stilts. In the previous century, heightened tensions were almost always military and observable only in the narrow no-man's land on the borders between countries. In recent decades, however, they have assumed more of a political character (less frequently, an economic or social character) and may be found wherever there are masses of people.

Heightened tensions are the adult form of conventional tensions—tensions that have acquired stilts by thriving on a rich diet of poverty, malnutrition, and especially alienation. Heightened tensions, like some other species in this Bestiary, exist only in the plural form and, rather than breed, seem to spring like maggots from the aforementioned dietary components. Their growth potential appears unlimited, and some analysts have reported heightened tensions heightening again and again.

64

*Bestiary*

Dire straits are another of nature's unpleasant beasties, notable primarily for their large mouths, voracious appetites, and penchant for ambushing the unwary. Frivolous governments, heedless of where they are treading, often find themselves suddenly in dire straits. Rescue is invariably difficult and unpleasant.*

Dire straits come in several genders, but dire economic straits are more common than the political, military, or social varieties. Dire straits are an

extremely social species: they always are observed in groups of two or more and never as a single strait. Nevertheless, they have never been observed to mate, and the method of their propagation remains a mystery.

---

* Viable alternatives are the natural enemies of dire straits. Governments escape dire straits when they have viable alternatives. The conflict is bloody, prolonged, and often seemingly in doubt. Although viable alternatives always prevail, the conflict is fatal to both parties.

65

*Bestiary*

The far-reaching implication is an animal that gov-ernments often ignore because of its odd physiognomy: its body tends to be ethereal, and most of its substance is concentrated in long mandibles, or arms. Governments are continually surprised to discover a far-reaching impli-cation reaching for something embarrassing or dangerous. Analysts seem to have a much better ability than govern-ments to discern far-reaching implications.

The far-reaching implication is the adolescent form of the conventional implication. As far-reaching implica-tions grow, their reach gradually shortens, and they become more visible, until they are easily seen by all and become mere implications. The loss of mandibles in this growth process is swift; no one, in fact, has ever observed a near-reaching implication.

66

*Bestiary*

One of the most awe-inspiring creatures is the available evidence, sometimes called the available information, which intelligence analysts frequently use to support shaky conclusions. This vital and difficult task is accomplished with utmost tact—"available evidence suggests . . ." The careless analyst sometimes asserts mistakenly that available evidence "indicates," not realizing that only full-fledged evidence can provide this degree of support. Analysts should be more appreciative of the available evidence's propping up ability and realize the difficulty they would be in without it.

As the name implies, available evidence is always nearby, whereas regular evidence may be off somewhere unaware that its presence is needed. A shy creature, an available evidence always slips away quietly once regular evidence arrives either to solidify the conclusion or sweep it away.

There was once a widely held view, now articulated only by purists, that available evidence is not a sub-species of evidence, that in fact there is only evidence or the lack thereof. Whatever evidence exists, they argue, is by definition available and, therefore, does not need to be so labeled. Modern research has disproved this myth, for we know now that unavailable evidence exists—it is somewhere else.

67

*Bestiary*

Foreseeable futures are the favorite pets of political and economic forecasters. No forecaster dares to be caught without one, and a forecaster with an obedient foreseeable future is admired by all.

They are moody and dangerous animals, however, and frequently turn upon their masters, causing them great public humiliation, derision, and grief. That such a disagreeable beast enjoys privileged status in society is testimony to its great prestige. The more professional futurists, however, such as weather

forecasters and most political analysts, have nothing to do with foreseeable futures. And, despite their name, these beasts are not suitable as seeing eye companions.

Most analysts, however, play around with regular futures, a less mercurial, related species that can still be misleading and dangerous. Economic analysts in particular often deal with pork belly futures and soy bean futures because of their occasional ability to sniff out hidden wealth. These futures, despite their names, are totally unrelated to foreseeable futures, although they are dangerous in their own right.

68

*Bestiary*

The almost inevitable, cousin to the virtually certain, is an indoor pest of the genus *eventuality* that has defied man's eradication efforts since the Dawn of Time. Curiously, many people have never seen an almost inevitable—because of its nocturnal habits—and some have labeled as almost inevitable things that really are not. The name has become synonymous with everything disagreeable—when faced with such prospects as death and taxes, people will throw up their hands and exclaim that "they're almost inevitable."

Some people argue, no doubt because it is so seldom seen, that the almost inevitable does not really exist. They maintain that the life cycle of the *eventuality* consists of only three stages—the possible, probable, and inevitable—and that there is no gradation between probable and inevitable. Some of our era's more thoughtful thinkers and editors, however, recognize the separate existence of the probably inevitable, a distinctive distinction that is lost on most people.

Such confusion is probably almost inevitable.

69

*Bestiary*

    Analysts and bookies are fond of ferreting out nonstarters, those unfortunate beasts that because of their physiognomy are destined never to enter, much less win, a contest. Their desire to compete is intense, however, and because of their marvelous faculty for disguise, they love to mingle with genuine starters and confuse the unwary. Journeymen analysts can quickly distinguish between starters and nonstarters: genuine starters have either wings so that they can fly or brass grommets so that they can be run up a flagpole and saluted. Congenital optimists, nonstarters are fond of consoling each other that they are merely ideas whose times have not yet come. In truth, however, they are often worn out or refurbished ideas and never were legitimate starters. One of nature's saddest species.

70

*Bestiary*

Economic constraints have become a common pest in the 1980s after being introduced into this country following World War II by soldiers returning from Europe. Infestations are thickest around institutes dealing with the "Dismal Science," but swarms of a new strain, tentatively called political constraints, have been mentioned in recent political and intelligence literature. Some Pentagon analysts and observers even report a possible third mutation, the military constraint.

Swarming constraints tend to produce clouds so dense as to obscure vision. Governments and individuals so beset have no choice but not to do whatever they were planning to do. Deceitful governments, anxious for an excuse not to do something, sometimes blame the arrival of a swarm of constraints for their inaction, when in fact there are no mites in the vicinity.

Impervious to weather, constraints can appear in any season. On the other hand, they rarely appear in political seasons, probably because candidates at such times do not want to imply that their vision and scope of action are at all limited. Constraints, curiously, seem to increase in activity after elections. Behaviorists also note that although constraints swarm in any season, they are directly affected by the economic (or political) climate, thriving when it is poor and disappearing when it is good.

71

*Bestiary*

Broad outlines are gluttonous predators that feed on the imaginations of professors, students, and political analysts. Unique in the zoological kingdom because they grow from the outside in, broad outlines are conventional in most

other ways— they are conceived and then carried to fruition unless they miscarry. As with humans, the process of conceiving broad outlines seems to be much more pleasurable than carrying them to fruition. There is a high infant mortality rate among broad outlines— they often fall prey to nonstarters—and many starve from lack of being filled in. Those that are lucky enough to be filled in discover, moreover, that people rapidly become more interested in the filling and quickly lose interest in the outlines.

Despite what their name implies, broad outlines do not share their phylum with what might be called narrow outlines. There are no such animals around today, nor is there any fossil evidence that any ever existed. The broad outlines' closest relatives are regular outlines, a modest, less impressive version. Broad outlines probably evolved out of regular outlines sometime in the past, the result of too rich a diet of academia nuts roasted in professorial hot air.

*Bestiary*

The net effect is a hybrid beast of burden developed by political scientists jealous of the net assessment that Secretary of Defense McNamara's "whiz kids" bred in the Pentagon basement in the early 1960s. The political analyst and his net effect quickly became an object of derision among economists and military analysts who looked down their noses at the beast as being too imprecise. In the last two decades, however, the net effect has popped up everywhere, and the net assessment is now found only in zoos and an occasional National Estimate.

The popularity of the net effect is obvious. Analysts quickly saw that its many long arms and legs would allow the net effect easily to wrap up data, draw bottom lines, summarize, conclude, and jump from fact to implication. Its genetic ancestor, the effect, could also do these things, but the addition of the net allowed the lazy and insecure analyst to imply more clearly to his supervisor that he was considering facts or trends on both sides of an issue.

The Russians are wont to claim discovery of the net effect, saying it is a contemporary manifestation of the thesis-antithesis-synthesis process discovered by Hegel and Marx which they apply scrupulously in solving all their problems. Until greater access to Soviet intelligence analysis allows an independent verification, this claim must be regarded as dubious.

73

*Bestiary*

The overwhelming majority is the best known of a species of draft animal used by many analysts to carry the burden of their argument and analysis. Its popularity stems from its versatility: it can believe, support, and advocate. It loves to vote, and polling organizations frequently cite it to support their conclusions. Garrulous and with an opinion on just about everything, overwhelming majorities seldom respond that they "have no opinion" or "don't know."

The species *majority* contains two sub-species: the *greater majority* (also known as the big or wide majority) and the *lesser majority* (sometimes called a narrow or thin majority). Overwhelming majorities are nothing more than overfed or overinflated *greater majorities*, which analysts mistakenly believe can do a job better because of their immense girth.* In fact, overwhelming majorities often tend to be flabby, and the most effective majority frequently is the leaner, tougher *working majority*.

---

* An overwhelming majority is called a consensus when it becomes so widespread that it is general. Perhaps for this reason some analysts occasionally talk about a general consensus. This is, of course, grossly inappropriate because contemporary consensuses are always anti-militaristic.

74

# CIA

The Central Intelligence Agency (CIA) is one of the principal intelligence-gathering agencies of the United States federal government. The CIA's headquarters is in Langley, Virginia, 2 miles (3.2 km) west of Washington, D.C. along the Potomac River. Its employees operate from U.S. embassies and many other locations around the world. Being the only independent U.S. intelligence agency, it reports to the Director of National Intelligence. The CIA has three traditional principal activities, which are gathering information about foreign governments, corporations, and individuals; analyzing that information, along with intelligence gathered by other U.S. intelligence agencies, in order to provide national security intelligence assessment to senior United States policymakers; and, upon the request of the President of the United States, carrying out or overseeing covert activities and some tactical operations by its own employees, by members of the U.S. military, or by other partners. It can, for example, exert foreign political influence through its tactical divisions, such as the Special Activities Division. In 2013, The Washington Post reported that the CIA had by far the largest budget in the Intelligence Community, exceeding previous estimates. The CIA has increasingly taken on offensive roles, including covert paramilitary operations. One of its largest divisions, the Information Operations Center (IOC), has shifted focus from counter-terrorism to offensive cyber-operations. Several CIA activities have attracted criticism. They include nonconsensual human experiments, extraordinary rendition, enhanced interrogation techniques (torture), targeted killings, assassinations and the funding and training of militants who would go on to kill civilians and non-combatants.

# Dr. Rube Goldberg

Fred Sanborn (November 23, 1899 – March 9, 1961) was an American vaudeville performer, actor, and musician. He was most notable as a member of Ted Healy's comedy troupe Ted Healy and his Southern Gentlemen (a group which included the trio that became the famous Three Stooges). Sanborn appeared frequently in the group's early stage acts. However, after appearing with Healy, Moe Howard, Larry Fine, and Shemp Howard in the Rube Goldberg film Soup to Nuts—for which Sanborn also wrote a song—he left the group, preferring to concentrate on his music rather than become known as a "Healyite". Sanborn's character was a quasi-Chaplinesque little fellow (completely with the lopsided walk) who is never heard speaking, preferring to whisper in other characters' ears while waggling his thick eyebrows. He appeared in films sporadically throughout the 1930s-40s, often in small, unspeaking comedy roles. His last performance was as a comedian on The Ed Wynn Show in 1950.

Ernests is a Latvian masculine given name. It is a cognate of the masculine given name Ernest and may refer to: Ernests Birznieks-Upītis (1871-1960), Latvian writer, translator and librarian Ernests Blanks (1894–1972), Latvian publicist, independence advocate Ernests Foldāts (1925–2003), Latvian-born Venezuelan botanist and orchidologist Ernests Gulbis (born 1988), Latvian professional tennis player Ernests Gūtmanis (1901-????), Latvian boxer and Olympic competitor Ernests Kalve (born 1987), professional basketball forward Ernests Štālbergs (1883–1958), Latvian architect Ernests Vīgners (1850-1933), Latvian composer and conductor

## Eugene McCarthy

Eugene Joseph "Gene" McCarthy (March 29, 1916 – December 10, 2005) was an American politician, poet, and a long-time member of the United States Congress from Minnesota. He served in the U.S. House of Representatives from 1949 to 1959 and the U.S. Senate from 1959 to 1971. In the 1968 presidential election, McCarthy was the first candidate to challenge incumbent Lyndon B. Johnson for the Democratic nomination for president of the United States, running on an anti-Vietnam War platform. The unexpected vote total he achieved in the New Hampshire primary and his strong polling in the upcoming Wisconsin primary led Johnson to withdraw from the race, and lured Robert F. Kennedy into the contest. Fellow Minnesotan US Vice-President Hubert Humphrey also entered the race after Johnson's withdrawal. McCarthy would unsuccessfully seek the presidency five times altogether.

## Forecasting

Forecasting is the process of making statements about events whose actual outcomes (typically) have not yet been observed. A commonplace example might be estimation of some variable of interest at some specified future date. Prediction is a similar, but more general term. Both might refer to formal statistical methods employing time series, cross-sectional or longitudinal data, or alternatively to less formal judgmental methods. Usage can differ between areas of application: for example, in hydrology, the terms "forecast" and "forecasting" are sometimes reserved for estimates of values at certain specific future times, while the term "prediction" is used for more general estimates, such as the number of times floods will occur over a long period. Risk and uncertainty are central to forecasting and prediction; it is generally considered good practice to indicate the degree of uncertainty attaching to forecasts. In any case, the data must be up to date in order for the forecast to be as accurate as possible.

## Gregor Mendel

Gregor Johann Mendel (20 July 1822 – 6 January 1884) was a German-speaking Moravian scientist and Augustinian friar who gained posthumous fame as the founder of the modern science of genetics. Though farmers had known for centuries that crossbreeding of animals and plants could favor certain desirable traits, Mendel's pea plant experiments conducted between 1856 and 1863 established many of the rules of heredity, now referred to as the laws of Mendelian inheritance. Mendel worked with seven characteristics of pea plants: plant height, pod shape and color, seed shape and color, and flower position and color. With seed color, he showed that when a yellow pea and a green pea were bred together their offspring plant was always yellow. However, in the next generation of plants, the green peas reappeared at a ratio of 1:3. To explain this phenomenon, Mendel coined the terms "recessive" and "dominant" in reference to certain traits. (In the preceding example, green peas are recessive and yellow peas are dominant.) He published his work in 1866, demonstrating the actions of invisible "factors"—now called genes—in providing for visible traits in predictable ways. The profound significance of Mendel's work was not recognized until the turn of the 20th century (more than three decades later) with the independent rediscovery of these laws. Erich von Tschermak, Hugo de Vries, Carl Correns, and William Jasper Spillman independently verified several of Mendel's experimental findings, ushering in the modern age of genetics.

# Hegel

Georg Wilhelm Friedrich Hegel (/ˈheɪɡəl/; German: [ˈgeɔʁk ˈvɪlhɛlm ˈfʁiːdʁɪç ˈheːɡəl]; August 27, 1770 – November 14, 1831) was a German philosopher who was a major figure in German idealism. His historicist and idealist account of reality revolutionized European philosophy and served as an important precursor to Continental philosophy, Marxism and historism. Hegel's principal achievement was his development of absolute idealism as a means to integrate the notions of mind, nature, subject, object, psychology, the state, history, art, religion and philosophy. In particular, he developed the notion of the master–slave dialectic and the concept of Geist ("mind-spirit") as the expression of the integration ("sublation", Aufheben), without elimination or reduction, of otherwise seemingly contradictory or opposing ideas. Examples include relationships between nature and freedom and between immanence and transcendence. He also made original and influential contributions to speculative logic, the role of history and the notions of the negative and the ethical. Hegel influenced many thinkers and writers whose own positions varied widely. Karl Barth described Hegel as a "Protestant Aquinas", while Maurice Merleau-Ponty wrote that "All the great philosophical ideas of the past century – the philosophies of Marx and Nietzsche, phenomenology, German existentialism, and psychoanalysis – had their beginnings in Hegel". Michel Foucault has contended that contemporary philosophers may be "doomed to find Hegel waiting patiently at the end of whatever road [they] travel".

# Intelligence Agency

An intelligence agency is a government agency responsible for the collection, analysis, and exploitation of information and intelligence in support of law enforcement, national security, defence and foreign policy objectives. Means of information gathering are both overt and covert and may include espionage, communication interception, cryptanalysis, cooperation with other institutions, and evaluation of public sources. The assembly and propagation of this information is known as intelligence analysis or intelligence assessment. Intelligence agencies can provide the following services for their national governments. Provision of analysis in areas relevant to national security; give early warning of impending crises; serve national and international crisis management by helping to discern the intentions of current or potential opponents; inform national defence planning and military operations; protect sensitive information secrets, both of their own sources and activities, and those of other state agencies; may act covertly to influence the outcome of events in favour of national interests, or influence international security; and Defence against the efforts of other national intelligence agencies (counter-intelligence). There is a distinction between "security intelligence" and "foreign intelligence". Security intelligence pertains to domestic threats (e.g. terrorism, espionage). Foreign intelligence involves information collection relating to the political, or economic activities of foreign states. Some agencies have been involved in assassination, arms trafficking, coups d'état, and the placement of misinformation (propaganda) as well as other covert operations, in order to support their own or their governments' interests.

## Intelligence Writing

Disorder of written expression is a type of learning disability in which a person's writing ability falls substantially below normally expected range based on the individual's age, educational background, and measured intelligence. Poor writing skills must interfere significantly with academic progress or daily activities that involves written expression (spelling, grammar, handwriting, punctuation, word usage, etc.). This disorder is also generally concurrent with disorders of reading and/or mathematics, as well as disorders related to behavior. Since it is so often associated with other learning disorders and mental problems, it is uncertain whether it can appear by itself. The prevalence of disorder of written expression is estimated to be of a similar frequency to other learning disorders, between 3 - 5%. A diagnosis can be made based on results of several assessments.

ves from a medieval variant of Geoffrey. Jeff is especially used in the USA and Canada.

## McNamara

Mac Conmara (anglicised as MacNamara or McNamara) is an Irish surname of a family of County Clare in Ireland. The MacNamara family were a Dál gCais sept and after the O'Briens one of the most powerful families in the Kingdom of Thomond as Lords of Clancullen (a title later divided into East and West families). They are related to the O'Gradys, also descended from the Uí Caisin line of the Dál gCais.

## mortality rate

Mortality rate, or death rate, is a measure of the number of deaths (in general, or due to a specific cause) in a particular population, scaled to the size of that population, per unit of time. Mortality rate is typically expressed in units of deaths per 1,000 individuals per year; thus, a mortality rate of 9.5 (out of 1,000) in a population of 1,000 would mean 9.5 deaths per year in that entire population, or 0.95% out of the total. It is distinct from the so-called "morbidity rate" (a vague term sometimes used to refer to either the prevalence or incidence of a disease), and also from the incidence rate (the number of newly appearing cases of the disease per unit of time).

## Pentagon

In geometry, a pentagon (from the Greek pente and gonia, meaning five and angle) is any five-sided polygon. A pentagon may be simple or self-intersecting. The sum of the internal angles in a simple pentagon is 540°. A pentagram is an example of a self-intersecting pentagon.

## political analyst

Political science is a social science discipline that deals with systems of government and the analysis of political activity and political behavior. It deals extensively with the theory and practice of politics which is commonly thought of as the determining of the distribution of power and resources. Political scientists "see themselves engaged in revealing the relationships underlying political events and conditions, and from these revelations they attempt to construct general principles about the way the world of politics works." Political science draws upon the fields of economics, law, sociology, history, anthropology, public administration, public policy, national politics, international relations, comparative politics, psychology, political organization, and political theory. Although it was codified in the 19th century, when all the social sciences were established, the study of political science has ancient roots that can be traced back to the works of Plato and Aristotle which were written nearly 2,500 years ago. Political science is commonly divided into distinct sub-disciplines which together constitute the field: political theory comparative politics public administration international relations public law political methodology Political theory is more concerned with contributions of various classical thinkers such as Aristotle, Niccolò Machiavelli, Cicero, Plato and many others. Comparative politics is the science of comparison and teaching of different types of constitutions, political actors, legislature and associated fields, all of them from an intrastate perspective. International relations deals with the interaction between nation-states as well as intergovernmental and transnational organizations. Political science is methodologically diverse and appropriates many methods originating in social research. Approaches include positivism, interpretivism, rational choice theory, behavioralism, structuralism, post-structuralism, realism, institutionalism, and pluralism. Political science, as one of the social sciences, uses methods and techniques that relate to the kinds of inquiries sought: primary sources such as historical documents and official records, secondary sources such as scholarly journal articles, survey research, statistical analysis, case studies, experimental research and model building.

## school of psychoanalysis

Boston Graduate School of Psychoanalysis was founded in 1973 as an institute to train psychoanalysts, particularly in the field of modern psychoanalysis.

## straits

A strait is a naturally formed, narrow, typically navigable waterway that connects two larger bodies of water. It most commonly refers to a channel of water that lies between two land masses, but it may also refer to a navigable channel through a body of water that is otherwise not navigable, for example because it is too shallow, or because it contains an unnavigable reef or archipelago.

## supervisor

Supervisor, foreman, foreperson, boss, overseer, cell coach, facilitator, or area coordinator is the job title of a low level management position that is primarily based on authority over a worker or charge of a workplace. The term itself can be used to refer to any personnel who have this task as part of their job description. An employee is a supervisor if he has the power and authority to do the following actions (according to the Ontario Ministry of Labour): Give instructions and/or orders to subordinates. Be held responsible for the work and actions of other employees. If an employee cannot do the above, legally, he or she is probably not a supervisor, but in some other category, such as lead hand. A supervisor is first and foremost an overseer whose main responsibility is to ensure that a group of subordinates get out the assigned amount of production, when they are supposed to do it and within acceptable levels of quality, costs and safety. A supervisor is responsible for the productivity and actions of a small group of employees. The supervisor has several manager-like roles, responsibilities, and powers. Two of the key differences between a supervisor and a manager are (1) the supervisor does not typically have "hire and fire" authority, and (2) the supervisor does not have budget authority. Lacking "hire and fire" authority means that a supervisor may not recruit the employees working in the supervisor's group nor does the supervisor have the authority to terminate an employee. The supervisor may participate in the hiring process as part of interviewing and assessing candidates, but the actual hiring authority rests in the hands of a Human Resource Manager. The supervisor may recommend to management that a particular employee be terminated and the supervisor may be the one who documents the behaviors leading to the recommendation but the actual firing authority rests in the hands of a manager. Lacking budget authority means that a supervisor is provided a budget developed by management within which constraints the supervisor is expected to provide a productive environment for the employees of the supervisor's work group. A supervisor will usually have the authority to make purchases within specified limits. A supervisor is also given the power to approve work hours and other payroll issues. Normally, budget affecting requests such as travel will require not only the supervisor's approval but the approval of one or more layers of management. As a member of management, a supervisor's main job is more concerned with orchestrating and controlling work rather than performing it directly.

# US Government

The government of the United States of America is the federal government of the republic of fifty states that constitute the United States, as well as one capital district, and several other territories. The federal government is composed of three distinct branches: legislative, executive and judicial, whose powers are vested by the U.S. Constitution in the Congress, the President, and the federal courts, including the Supreme Court, respectively. The powers and duties of these branches are further defined by acts of Congress, including the creation of executive departments and courts inferior to the Supreme Court. The full name of the republic is "The United States of America". No other name appears in the Constitution, and this is the name that appears on money, in treaties, and in legal cases to which it is a party (e.g., Charles T. Schenck v. United States). The terms "Government of the United States of America" or "United States Government" are often used in official documents to represent the federal government as distinct from the states collectively. In casual conversation or writing, the term "Federal Government" is often used, and the term "National Government" is sometimes used. The terms "Federal" and "National" in government agency or program names generally indicate affiliation with the federal government (e.g., Federal Bureau of Investigation, National Oceanic and Atmospheric

Administration, etc.). Because the seat of government is in Washington, D.C., "Washington" is commonly used as a metonym for the federal government.

# World War II

World War II (WWII or WW2), also known as the Second World War (after the recent Great War), was a global war that lasted from 1939 to 1945, though related conflicts began earlier. It involved the vast majority of the world's nations—including all of the great powers—eventually forming two opposing military alliances: the Allies and the Axis. It was the most widespread war in history, and directly involved more than 100 million people from over 30 countries. In a state of "total war", the major participants threw their entire economic, industrial and scientific capabilities behind the war effort, erasing the distinction between civilian and military resources. Marked by mass deaths of civilians, including the Holocaust (during which approximately 11 million people were killed) and the strategic bombing of industrial and population centres (during which approximately one million people were killed, including the use of two nuclear weapons in combat), it resulted in an estimated 50 million to 85 million fatalities. These made World War II the deadliest conflict in human history. The Empire of Japan aimed to dominate Asia and the Pacific and was already at war with the Republic of China in 1937, but the world war is generally said to have begun on 1 September 1939 with the invasion of Poland by Germany and subsequent declarations of war on Germany by France and the United Kingdom. From late 1939 to early 1941, in a series of campaigns and treaties, Germany conquered or controlled much of continental Europe, and formed the Axis alliance with Italy and Japan. Following the Molotov–Ribbentrop Pact, Germany and the Soviet Union partitioned and annexed territories of their European neighbours, including Poland, Finland and the Baltic states. The United Kingdom and the British Commonwealth were the only Allied forces continuing the fight against the Axis, with campaigns in North Africa and the Horn of Africa as well as the long-running Battle of the Atlantic. In June 1941, the European Axis powers launched an invasion of the Soviet Union, opening the largest land theatre of war in history, which trapped the major part of the Axis' military forces into a war of attrition. In December 1941, Japan attacked the United States and European territories in the Pacific Ocean, and quickly conquered much of the Western Pacific. The Axis advance halted in 1942 when Japan lost the critical Battle of Midway, near Hawaii, and Germany was defeated in North Africa and then, decisively, at Stalingrad in the Soviet Union. In 1943, with a series of German defeats on the Eastern Front, the Allied invasion of Italy which brought about Italian surrender, and Allied victories in the Pacific, the Axis lost the initiative and undertook strategic retreat on all fronts. In 1944, the Western Allies invaded France, while the Soviet Union regained all of its territorial losses and invaded Germany and its allies. During 1944 and 1945 the Japanese suffered major reverses in mainland Asia in South Central China and Burma, while the Allies crippled the Japanese Navy and captured key Western Pacific islands. The war in Europe ended with an invasion of Germany by the Western Allies and the Soviet Union culminating in the capture of Berlin by Soviet and Polish troops and the subsequent German unconditional surrender on 8 May 1945. Following the Potsdam Declaration by the Allies on 26 July 1945, the United States dropped atomic bombs on the Japanese cities of Hiroshima and Nagasaki on 6 August and 9 August respectively. With an invasion of the Japanese archipelago imminent, the possibility of additional atomic bombings, and the Soviet Union's declaration of war on Japan and invasion of Manchuria, Japan surrendered on 15 August 1945. Thus ended the war in Asia, and the final destruction of the Axis bloc. World War II altered the political alignment and social structure of the world. The United Nations (UN) was established to foster international co-operation and prevent future conflicts. The victorious great powers—the United States, the Soviet Union, China, the United Kingdom, and France—became the permanent members of the United Nations Security Council. The Soviet Union and the United States emerged as rival superpowers, setting the stage for the Cold War, which lasted for the next 46 years. Meanwhile, the influence of European great powers waned, while the decolonisation of Asia and Africa began. Most countries whose industries had been damaged moved towards economic recovery. Political integration, especially in Europe, emerged as an effort to end pre-war enmities and to create a common identity.

www.ingramcontent.com/pod-product-compliance
Lightning Source LLC
Chambersburg PA
CBHW080736290526
45790CB00008B/3212